Virtual Reality in Logistics and Supply Chain Management

Increasing Efficiency

Table of Contents

Chapter 1. Introduction

In this Special Report, we will delve into an exciting, burgeoning field of technology that is poised to redefine the parameters of Logistics and Supply Chain Management - Virtual Reality (VR). Don't let the term "VR" intimidate you! Even though it may sound like the stuff of science fiction, our report breaks it down into simple terms everyone can understand. This technology has metamorphosed into a practical tool with sweeping implications for the logistics sector. The significant enhancements in efficiency, increased precision in processes, and tangible improvements in productivity are all fruits of integrating VR in daily operations. If you're curious about how these technological advancements are remodeling various logistic flows, consider this comprehensive report your go-to resource. It promises to shed light on the exciting opportunities presented by VR, aiming to pique your curiosity, provide strategic insights, and offer actionable recommendations to infuse new vigor in your logistical workflows. Simply put, it's an investment that is sure to pay its dividends in enriched knowledge and strategic foresight!

Chapter 2. Demystifying Virtual Reality: A Primer

Virtual reality, or VR as it's more commonly known, has evolved from a fringe technological concept into a mainstream technology with profound implications for many industries, including Logistics and Supply Chain Management. This first chapter aims to make VR accessible and meaningful to all readers by stripping away the complexity and introducing the world of virtual reality in clear, straightforward terms.

2.1. What is Virtual Reality?

In the most simplistic terms, Virtual Reality (VR) is a simulated experience that can resemble reality or diverge significantly from it. It refers to a computer-generated simulation in which a person can interact within an artificial three-dimensional environment using electronic devices, such as special goggles with a screen or gloves fitted with sensors.

2.2. VR: A Brief History

The concept of VR has a deeper and more diverse history than many realize. The pioneering works that led to what we now understand as VR can be traced back to the mid-nineteenth century with the advent of 360-degree murals. However, the first use of the term "Virtual Reality" was not until the late 1980s, credited to Jaron Lanier, the founder of the visual programming lab (VPL).

During the 1990s, developments took a significant leap forward with the emergence of VR arcade games and VR helmets designed for home use. The 2000s saw the technology become more sophisticated, with the creation of Google street view offering a comprehensive VR walking tour. Today, we can easily access VR technology on personal computers, with companies like Oculus, HTC, and Sony leading the charge.

2.3. Understanding the Core Components of VR

At its core, VR comprises several interlinked components:

1. Hardware: This includes devices like VR headsets, gloves, and motion sensors that help translate real-world movements into digital actions.

2. Software: VR software creates the artificial environments and objects that users interact with. These can range from realistic simulations of the real world to fantastical landscapes that defy the laws of physics.

3. User Experience: A crucial aspect of VR lies in creating a realistic and immersive experience. This involves carefully calibrating the user's sensory feedback to the actions they perform in the simulated environment, giving the illusion of "presence".

2.4. The Mechanics of VR

The functioning of VR technologies hinges on two key aspects:

1. Immersion: This is the degree to which the user feels they are part of the artificial environment. True immersion involves stimulating multiple senses, not just sight and sound.

2. Interaction: The level of interaction refers to how users can manipulate their environment or perform actions within it. High levels of interaction typically require special equipment like gloves or handheld controllers with motion sensors.

2.5. The Pervasiveness of VR in Everyday Life

Even though the term VR still might sound futuristic to many, it's surprisingly more embedded in our everyday lives than we usually recognize. For instance, simplistic VR tools are being used in industries such as real estate, where potential home buyers can take 360-degree virtual tours of houses. In the medical sector, VR assists in planning complicated surgeries or in providing training to medical students. In the military, it's used for flight simulation and battlefield scenarios for training purposes.

2.6. VR Applications In Logistics and Supply Chain Management

The logistic and supply chain sector is on the brink of a radical transformation, with VR at the heart of it. From enhancing inventory management to assisting in forklift operations, VR poses several distinct advantages. Advanced VR tools help simulate different warehousing scenarios or logistics planning, which aid in arriving at optimized solutions. These are just a taste of what's to come, with the opportunities VR presents to the logistics sector being vast and diversified.

2.7. The Road Ahead

Even though VR has come a long way, its full potential is yet to be harnessed. The road ahead is exciting, albeit loaded with challenges to be overcome, especially in terms of making the technology affordable and easily adaptable. However, as the VR landscape matures, so too will its applications multiply, especially in sectors like logistics, where operational efficiency and precision are paramount.

This chapter aimed to unravel the intriguing world of VR and provide a foundation on which subsequent chapters will build. As we move through this report, we'll delve deeper into the specifics of how VR technology is propelling the logistics and supply chain industry towards a future of unparalleled efficiency and precision. The journey is just beginning!

Chapter 3. Exploring the Intersection of VR and Logistics

As we embark on investigating the overlapping domains of VR and logistics, it helps to understand the capabilities of the VR technology and how it is significantly changing the operations landscape in the logistics sector.

Virtual Reality, commonly referred to as VR, is a powerful technology that creates a simulated environment, immersing its users in a three-dimensional setting and mimics the physical world functionality in a digital environment. VR employs specially created hardware and software to emulate a highly interactive and authentic environment, which is particularly effective in simulating situational experiences.

3.1. The Increasing Popularity of VR

The adoption of VR has soared in the past years due to its increasing affordability and accessibility. According to Statista, the VR market size is expected to reach a whopping 16 billion USD by 2022, a steep rise from the estimated market size of 6.1 billion USD in 2016. Its vast range of applications – extending from gaming and entertainment to training and education, real estate, engineering, and many more – explains this popularity.

In the logistics sector, VR is fast becoming a game-changer, re-engineering operations, drive up efficiencies, and boost productivity.

3.2. How VR is Reshaping the Logistics Sector

The logistics sector has invariably been a realm of consistency and routinized processes. However, the inclusion of VR is disrupting this pattern and redefining how logistic operations are carried out.

One of the primary ways through which VR is transforming the logistics sector is through training. VR-powered training simulations offer an immersive experience for a variety of roles ranging from forklift operators to cargo inspectors. These VR applications can mimic specific workplace environments and conditions, allowing users to understand the workings on the ground without being physically present at the location.

In the warehouse management domain, VR is used to map 3D models of warehouse layouts. This affords managers an aerial view of the warehouse infrastructure, assists in identifying bottlenecks, and optimize workflows.

3.3. Case Studies: VR in Practice

Distinct logistics operators have already begun leveraging VR capabilities to their advantage. DHL, for instance, has successfully piloted a training program using VR. They experimentally introduced VR-powered training for their staff, reducing the onboarding process by half and ramping up productivity by 15%.

Similarly, UPS also uses VR to train their delivery vehicle drivers to handle real-world situations. They offer Virtual Reality driving simulations that assist their employees in understanding and managing logistical challenges (e.g., lane changing, deciphering signs) without the risk of real-life trials.

3.4. Looking Towards the Future

With VR adoption on an upsurge in the logistics sector, the future promises more radical transformations. From offering hyper-detailed augmented reality instructions for warehouse workers, facilitating remote troubleshooting for mechanical issues, to simulating emergency scenarios for training purposes - the potential implementations seem boundless.

Advancements in AI and machine learning algorithms will additionally complement these VR potentials, leading to the development of even more intelligent systems that can augment decision making and coordinate autonomous logistic operations.

3.5. The Role of VR in Supply Chain Management

Not only restricted to logistics, VR holds impactful potential in enhancing supply chain processes too. From tracking and tracing shipments in real-time, ensuring product quality, managing inventory, to offering the capacity to unseal and inspect individual packages remotely - VR affords capabilities to improve the transparency and visibility within the supply chain.

3.6. Final Thoughts

The advent of VR in the logistics sector opens up a world of new operational efficiencies, productivity enhancements, and opportunities for reorganization. Keeping abreast of the curve, understanding its implications, and implementing it to augment existing systems can provide logistic companies a robust competitive advantage in the market.

However, increased adoption coupled with the rapid pace of

technology might also give rise to newer challenges such as cyber risks and data privacy issues, thereby demanding ample cyber resilience measures.

Embracing change is an integral part of staying competitive in the fluctuating business dynamics. With the surging digital transition, inclusion of VR technologies is not just an innovative development but entails an imminent change. By understanding the technologies at our disposal, we can navigate and mold these transformations to our advantage, ensuring an agile, flexible, and strong logistics sector for the future.

Chapter 4. The Role of VR in Warehouse Management

Integrated with IoT sensors and AI, virtual reality (VR) is quickly becoming a game changer in warehouse management. This technology's potential to revolutionize warehousing flows, improve inventory tracking, and develop employee training is transforming traditional logistics management.

4.1. VR and Warehousing Flows

Virtual reality (VR) is fundamentally reshaping the traditional patterns of warehousing flows. By visualizing the entire supply chain, warehouse managers can simulate optimal routes and procedures holistically before implementing them.

One primary application of VR in warehousing flows involves planning and layout design. By creating a virtual representation of the warehouse space, managers can experiment with countless configurations without physical alteration. They can use VR devices to move virtual pallets around or change shelving configurations with a simple swipe or voice command.

Additionally, VR is instrumental in identifying bottlenecks within the supply chain. It can simulate high-demand periods to analyze the efficiency of warehouse flows, allowing managers to make preemptive changes to avoid real-time operational disruptions.

4.2. Improved Inventory Tracking

From tracking merchandise to maintaining an updated inventory, VR can handle an array of administrative tasks in warehousing.

Traditional inventory management often relies on manual data entry, prone to errors. However, VR provides a foolproof method, creating virtual duplicates of items as they are delivered and removed from the warehouses. The technology records and updates this information in the cloud database in real-time, providing accurate, consistent inventory tracking.

VR also simplifies the process of locating items in the warehouse. Integrated with AI and IoT, VR headsets can promptly guide employees to the location of the required items–thus expediting the order preparation process and reducing the chances of misplacement or loss.

4.3. Transforming Employee Training

A crucial challenge in warehouse management is to train employees and reduce the learning curve and associated costs. VR is proving to be an invaluable tool here.

Using VR, organizations can create engaging training modules using realistic scenarios, allowing new employees to gain hands-on experience without the risk associated with handling actual equipment or goods. This not only enhances learning efficacy but also ensures safety during the learning phase.

Moreover, VR training is cost-effective. It negates the need for warehouses to be shut down for training sessions or for actual merchandise to be used in training - reducing damage risks and losses.

4.4. Warehouse Safety with VR

Improved safety is another benefit offered by VR to the warehousing industry. Managers can visualize the warehouse layout and integrate safety measures before the real implementation - eliminating potential risks.

Moreover, VR simulations can help reiterate safety procedures and protocols to the workforce. This allows for an efficient way of addressing and dealing with potential hazardous situations, minimizing accidents, and ensuring the safety of the employees.

4.5. VR's Role in Future Warehousing

While VR's present impact on warehousing is significant, its future potential is even more promising. With advancements in technology, VR integrated with AI, IoT, and other technologies will make warehouses more efficient and safe.

In the upcoming trends, VR could facilitate remote warehouse management, allowing managers to oversee operations from a distance. Furthermore, it could potentially lead to autonomous warehouses run by robots, where human intervention would be limited to a minimum.

Overall, the rapid progression in VR technology is continually opening up new opportunities in warehouse management. It holds the promise for a more streamlined, efficient, and productive warehousing industry.

In closing, the utility of VR extends well beyond warehouse management; it touches upon while creating new horizons for innovation in logistics and supply chain management. The logistics sector needs to leverage these technological advancements for effective, efficient, and futuristic operations.

Chapter 5. Freight Transportation Redefined: The VR Perspective

In order to highlight the transformative power of Virtual Reality (VR) in transforming freight transportation, we must first understand the current scope, challenges, and limitations of traditional freight transportation systems.

Today, the world has become increasingly interconnected. Global supply chains, powered by expansive freight networks, are the highways that foster this connectivity. Although we have made significant strides in optimizing freight logistics, the sector is still riddled with inefficiencies. Freight transportation, in its traditional sense, lacks real-time data accuracy, visibility, and effective human-resource management, to name a few.

Virtual Reality (VR) paves a pathway for transcending these limitations, thus redefining freight transportation.

5.1. The Mechanism of VR in Freight Transportation

The beauty of VR lies in its potential to bridge the gap between the digital and the physical world. Adopting VR in freight transport equates to creating an interactive, digital environment that accurately represents real-world processes. It allows users to perceive, interact with, and manipulate these processes in a way that was previously deemed impossible.

5.2. Real-time Data and Network Visibility

One of the key aspects where VR can significantly influence freight transportation is facilitating real-time data visibility. Traditionally, data related to shipments is updated manually, often leading to inaccuracies and delays. With VR, you could potentially visualize your whole network in digital form, with real-time updates on every cargo's status. This instant network visibility would foster more effective decision-making processes across the supply chain.

5.3. Training and Skill Enhancement

VR can also serve as a powerful tool for human resource development in the freight industry. Virtual Reality training simulators, for drivers and operators, can offer a safe and controlled environment to practice various freight handling operations. These include loading and unloading of shipments, managing cargo on vessels, and dealing with emergency situations. As a result, the workforce becomes more skilled, efficient, and better equipped to handle real-life challenges.

5.4. Efficiency Through VR-based Process Optimization

By introducing VR, freight transportation processes can be tested and optimized in a risk-free, cost-effective manner. Logistics managers can digitally orchestrate freight movement and identify potential bottlenecks or inefficiencies. They can then modify these processes, in a digital environment first, before implementing changes in the real world. It becomes possible to verify the effects of changes without actual implementations and their consequential costs, thus enhancing overall efficiency.

5.5. How VR Strengthens Safety Protocols

Implicit in the nature of freight transportation is an array of potential hazards - ranging from accidents to damage of goods in transit. VR allows for a better understanding and designing of safety protocols in an immersive learning environment, thereby minimizing accidents and improving safety standards.

5.6. Enabling Interconnected Freight Networks

As we move closer to the reality of globally interconnected freight networks, the role of VR in making this dream a reality becomes more eminent. VR can aid in the design, testing, and optimization of an interconnected global network, ensuring its smooth operation while managing disruption risks.

5.7. Final Thoughts

The breakthroughs of VR in the world of freight transportation necessitate a shift in our perspectives. This shift, though initially challenging, has the potential to bring about radical improvements - flattening inefficiencies, enhancing safety, refining skills, and opening up avenues of unimaginable optimization.

As we embrace VR, we redefine freight transportation for a world woven by ceaseless interconnectivity, bringing us steps closer to a future where distances become irrelevant, and efficiency becomes the norm.

Virtual Reality is more than a technological marvel; it's a shift in operational paradigms and a leap towards an efficient, interconnected future. The sooner we realize its potential, the sooner we can harness its power to transform the world of freight transportation.

Chapter 6. Innovation in Inventory Management through VR

The impacts of virtual reality (VR) in modern commerce are becoming increasingly apparent, with one of the most noteworthy applications being inventory management. The innovative use of VR in managing inventory signals a major shift in how logistics are approached and serves to underscore the dynamic potential of this technology.

6.1. Applying VR to Inventory Management

Virtual Reality has introduced innovative ways to manage inventories, coalescing novelty with effectiveness. VR allows companies to simulate their warehouses in a 3D virtual environment, creating an interactive digital twin of the real-world facility. This digital environment facilitates experimentation with different layouts and storage strategies without causing any tangible impacts on daily operations, which is a significant advantage over traditional methods.

In standard operations, rearrangements or strategic changes to layouts often lead to temporary inaccuracies and inefficient use of resources. VR eliminates this issue by providing an avenue to test these changes virtually before any real-world application. The possibility of refining layouts and strategies in VR decreases errors, optimizes storage, and enhances the overall efficiency of warehouse operations.

6.2. VR for Data Visualization and Analysis

Notably, VR serves as a powerful tool for data visualization. Within the VR environment, data related to inventory management can be represented as interactive 3D models. This approach offers high visibility into inventory status and storage locations, enabling staff to locate items swiftly and decreasing the time taken for picking operations.

Compared to plain spreadsheets or databases, VR allows for a much more immersive and realistic representation of data. For example, managers can visualize stock levels in real-time, identify patterns, and anticipate future requirements. Consequently, this leads to increased foresight, aiding in inventory level optimization and demand forecasting.

6.3. Enhancing Employee Training

VR has shown substantial promise in employee training, especially in inventory management. Traditionally, training new employees on the inventory management system is cost-intensive and time-consuming. However, VR offers a novel solution by providing an immersive environment closely resembling real-world conditions, thereby facilitating effective hands-on learning.

With VR, new hires can be trained in a controlled environment to correct any inefficiencies or errors without real-world implications. It contributes to accelerating the learning process, reducing the possibility of mistakes, and significantly trimming down training costs.

6.4. Integrating VR with other Technologies

VR doesn't operate in isolation. It often works best in conjunction with other technologies like Artificial Intelligence (AI) or Internet of Things (IoT). For instance, integrating VR with AI can automate certain aspects of inventory management, such as restocking inventory levels or maintaining optimal temperature conditions.

IoT devices can be used to track, record, and transmit data about goods in real-time to the VR environment. This integration offers higher accuracy in tracking goods, ensuring efficient inventory control, and reducing shrinkage.

6.5. Challenges and Solutions

Despite the potential benefits, the integration of VR into inventory management is not without challenges. Firstly, cost can be a limiting factor, especially for small to medium-sized businesses. However, with VR technology becoming increasingly affordable, this barrier is gradually being eroded.

Secondly, the complexity of implementing VR solutions may intimidate some businesses. Yet, this is where strategic partnerships with technology providers become valuable. These partnerships ensure that VR solutions are tailored to business needs and are implemented seamlessly.

Lastly, getting employees comfortable with using VR in everyday operations could present a hurdle. This challenge can be overcome by providing adequate training. Furthermore, employees can gradually transition to using VR systems by initially integrating them within small segments of their daily routine.

6.6. The Future of Inventory Management: Embracing VR

In the fast-paced global economy, leveraging technology to streamline inventory management is becoming crucial. As seen, VR presents a compelling case for its inclusion in inventory management operations. From enhancing data visualization to streamlining employee training, VR is set to drastically redefine the parameters of inventory management.

By approaching VR integration strategically, businesses stand to benefit immensely. The time to embrace VR is now, and it promises to revolutionize inventory management in ways previously unimaginable. As we move forward, firms should anticipate the paradigm shift and prepare to adapt to remain a step ahead in the competitive business landscape. Virtual Reality is not merely a futuristic concept; it's the new reality of business operations.

Chapter 7. Improving Training and Safety Measures with Virtual Reality

VR's blend of virtual and physical worlds makes it an innovative tool for training and safety measures in logistics. It provides realistic, immersive environments for workers to familiarize themselves with critical processes and complex operations without the usual risks associated with traditional training methods.

7.1. Exploring the Use of VR in Training

VR technology enables interactive and immersive training. It allows learners to gain firsthand experience and practice in a safe, controlled, virtual environment. This method is superior to traditional training programs, which often involve direct handling of equipment or navigating complex logistical operations with potential for errors. VR also eliminates costs associated with physical training resources, time taken to set up realistic training environments or potential loss due to accidental damage.

For instance, a worker in a warehouse can use VR to engage in a simulated task of operating a forklift. The operator can practice repetitively, honing skills while minimizing the risk of accidents. The process increases their confidence level before they handle real-life operations.

Moreover, the use of VR is scalable. A single program can be deployed across various regions simultaneously, reducing the costs and logistical issues associated with conventional training methods.

Thus, utilizing VR for training not only enhances employees' skills but also significantly cuts down on operational costs and potential risks.

7.2. Safety Implementation Through VR

Virtual reality is a powerful tool for enforcing safety measures in logistics. Dangerous situations, from manual handling injuries to accidents involving heavy machinery, can be simulated in detail with VR, which provides a firsthand experience of the hazards and their potential impact. Safety training through VR is not passive like traditional methods, rather it's an immersive experience that enables retention of information and encourages safer behavior in the workplace.

Using VR, companies can simulate a variety of accidental situations and showcase the resulting aftermath which otherwise would be impossible to experience in real life. This sensory stimulation and real-time feedback drastically drive home the importance of safety protocols and adherence to guidelines.

7.3. Application and Case Studies

Let's consider the case of DHL, the world's leading mail and logistics company. DHL Express has been utilizing virtual reality to train its employees in cargo loading and unloading, safety procedures, and emergency protocols. Through VR, DHL has managed to enhance its employee's confidence and capabilities in managing routine tasks and exigencies while ensuring a higher level of safety.

In a similar vein, UPS, the multinational package delivery and supply chain management company, uses VR to train its drivers. The virtual environment simulates urban and rural routes and a variety of challenges the drivers may encounter, allowing them to learn and adapt in a risk-free setting.

7.4. Efficiency and Time Saving

With VR, training tasks can be split into several short modules, which are more manageable and far less disruptive than traditional training programs that often require longer uninterrupted periods. This modular training ensures employees can learn at their own pace and in a more focused manner, making the training more effective overall.

Companies can customize virtual reality training scenarios according to their specific needs, accurately reflecting the realities of their working environment. This hyper-relevant training further boosts productivity and performance, as employees are better equipped to handle the exact challenges they may face during their daily operations.

7.5. Future Scope

Looking ahead, the role of VR in training and safety measures in logistics will only grow more substantial. As technology advances, VR will become more immersive, detailed, and tailored to suit various logistic functions. It can help introduce workers to a wide array of scenarios, operations, and potential hazards, preparing them to navigate real-world challenges skillfully and safely.

In conclusion, VR offers an effective, immersive, and engaging method for training and safety measures in logistics. Its use can reduce costs, increase efficiency, improve worker safety, and enhance overall productivity. A critical tool for the future, VR will continue to revolutionize logistics training, offering an unparalleled opportunity for growth, development and safety assurance.

Chapter 8. Applications of VR in Packaging and Handling

To fully appreciate the profound impacts of VR technology in packaging and handling, it's crucial to dissect it well and understand its various manifestations. This includes specific use cases, projects that have demonstrated the potential of VR, evolving trends in its applications, and future forecasts that envisage the shift in packaging and handling paradigms.

8.1. Understanding The Realm of VR in Packaging and Handling

Virtual Reality (VR) applications are increasingly utilized in the logistics sector, including packaging and handling. This technology helps logistics companies simulate complex processes and create a digital twin of the physical world to improve efficiency, accuracy, and safety in operations. VR can be a game-changer in packaging and handling as it enables companies to visualize packaging designs, plan more precise and efficient handling processes, rehearse operations without logistical constraints, and analyze results to continuously improve upon the methods implemented.

In the packaging and handling sector, VR opens up a multitude of possibilities. It significantly aids with visualizing packaging designs and product placements. Designers can now examine their creations in a 3D environment before the physical version is produced. This saves considerable time, cost, and resources that would otherwise be spent on trial and error. Moreover, VR allows real-time feedback, which further empowers designers to refine their designs optimally.

The other area that benefits immensely from VR is the handling process. Thanks to VR, operators can now practice their tasks in a zero-risk virtual environment. This not only improves their skills but also increases their confidence, inevitably leading to increased efficiency and safety at work.

8.2. Successfully Leveraged VR Projects

Several innovative projects successfully demonstrate the transformative power of VR in packaging and handling. One such instance is the BMW Group, which uses VR to simulate packaging processes. By creating virtual copies of actual workstations, BMW provides its workers with a 3D vision of how the process will unfold, allowing them to create efficient workflows and identify potential issues in advance. Not only has this led to a reduction in errors in the packaging process, but it also significantly speeds up the process itself.

Another noteworthy project is the use of VR by DHL for training in the concept of 'pick and pack.' Here, the employees go through a VR module that simulates the entire picking and packing process. It significantly reduces the training time, and the workers are more prepared for real-life scenarios in the warehouse.

8.3. Emerging Trends and Future Realities

The future holds immense promise for VR in packaging and handling. With advancements in technology, one can envisage a future where VR will play an even more critical role. For instance, tacit learning - learning through immersive experience rather than formal teaching, will become more commonplace. We can also anticipate a wider integration with other technologies like the Internet of Things (IoT) to create more hybrid solutions.

Moreover, as VR headsets become lighter and more comfortable, their acceptance will increase, leading to an even wider adoption. You can expect to see more innovations centered around haptic technology too, which will further enhance the VR experience by providing a tactile response.

Also, there's the concept of 'remote handling' that's gaining traction. Here, an operator can control a machine or process remotely using VR, reducing the physical risks associated with certain tasks.

8.4. Actionable Recommendations

Given the clear benefits and the significant potential, companies must seriously consider integrating VR into their packaging and handling workflows. Some of the actionable steps to be considered are:

1. Begin with small-scale pilot programs that demonstrate the capabilities of VR before scaling up.

2. Collaborate with VR solution providers and ensure the technology is tailored to unique business requirements.

3. Regularly upskill and retrain the workforce to handle VR technology.

4. Always stay informed about the latest developments in the field of VR to maximize the competitive advantage.

In conclusion, the applications of VR in packaging and handling are vast, touching every aspect of the process - from concept and design to execution and supervision. As VR continues to mature, its role will only become more pivotal, prompting businesses to keep pace with technological enhancements and the benefits they herald. While reskilling their labor force remains a significant challenge, the advantages VR brings in terms of enhanced efficiency, better designs, safer environments, and cost savings are compelling enough to prompt businesses to adopt and adapt.

Chapter 9. Case Studies: Lessons from Early Adopters of VR

Virtual Reality, or VR, has seen leaps and strides in application across various industries, thanks to its innate ability to simulate real-world situations in a controlled setting. The logistics industry stands as one of the major benefactors of this technological evolution, as a handful of pioneering firms have adopted and integrated VR solutions into their operations. The following case studies offer rich insights into how these early adopters of VR have innovated their processes and gained significant advantages.

9.1. Walmart: Training with Virtual Reality

Walmart stands as one of the prime examples of companies leveraging the power of VR for operational efficiency. The retail giant decided to deploy VR in 2017 as a part of its Walmart Academy training program, aiming to equip employees with better decision-making skills during critical situations which can be challenging to recreate.

Strivr, a startup spearheading the VR training landscape, developed customized training modules for Walmart, simulating situations like peak-hour rush, dealing with unhappy customers, or cleaning up spills. These immersive simulations provided a safe and controlled environment for the employees to learn from, equipping them to better handle real-world scenarios. The result was impressive improvements in employees' performance and decision-making, reinforcing the value proposition of VR in large-scale operations.

9.2. DHL: Enhancing Order Picking Process

DHL, one of the world's leading logistics companies, piloted a program with "smart glasses" to streamline the order picking process. The glasses, equipped with VR technology, provided visual displays of order picking instructions along with information on where items are located and where they need to be placed on the cart.

In this case, VR served as a means to eliminate manual processes and reduce errors, effectively enhancing productivity and efficiency. DHL reported a 25% increase in efficiency during the pilot project, highlighting the potential of integrating VR into supply chains.

9.3. Kuehne + Nagel: Implementing VR for Dangerous Goods Training

Kuehne + Nagel employed VR to train their staff in handling dangerous goods. By simulating hazardous materials incidents, the company provided a safer training method that mitigates risks. It also meant that employees could train for these situations without having to be physically present, reducing travel times and costs.

Furthermore, the regularity of the training could be increased due to the ease of accessibility, leading to better-prepared employees and a reduced risk of danger when handling hazardous materials. The company's use of VR technology emphasizes not only its utility for efficiency but also as a tool for safety mitigation in high-risk scenarios.

9.4. UPS: Driving Training with VR

Upskilling delivery drivers is a top priority for United Parcel Service (UPS). The multinational company adopted VR for driver training in 2017. VR headsets simulate the experience of driving on city streets while teaching the users to spot and identify potential hazards. A key value of this training is the ability to simulate diverse scenarios that a driver can encounter, thereby offering comprehensive training.

UPS found that VR-trained drivers had shorter training times and better retention rates compared to traditional methods. This move was a testament to the significant role VR can play in reducing training costs and improving service quality in supply chain management.

These case studies validate the application of VR in creating a more efficient, productive, and savvy logistics workforce. From training to core operations, VR is providing a disruptive solution to traditional methods. Early adopters are already reaping the benefits, paving the way for broader scale adoption across the logistics and supply chain landscape.

Chapter 10. Overcoming Barriers to VR Adoption in Supply Chain Management

Although Virtual Reality (VR) technology offers a broad range of promising applications and benefits to the logistics and supply chain sector, its adoption is not without challenges. This section explores the various barriers to VR adoption in this sector, offers potential strategies for overcoming these barriers, and highlights how early adopters have managed to cut through the hurdles.

10.1. Understanding the Tech

One of the formidable hurdles in the way of VR integration in supply chain management is the lack of understanding of the technology. It's a leap from traditional supply chain processes, and a lack of adequate technical knowledge can hinder its adoption.

To combat this, companies can invest in training programs and workshops designed to introduce staff to VR technology. They can use a gradual learning approach, starting with the basics and gradually introducing more sophisticated applications. Furthermore, organizations can also leverage partnerships with tech firms specializing in VR development to provide more focused training and support.

10.2. High Initial Investment

The initial cost of integrating VR technology into existing systems can be daunting. VR hardware, software, and the necessary infrastructure doesn't come cheap. Also, the costs associated with staff training add to the financial challenges.

However, focusing solely on the initial costs fails to consider the long-term returns. Higher efficiency, precise processes, and improved productivity that VR brings can fast offset those initial costs. Additionally, the continual drop in the prices of VR equipment and progression in open-source VR solutions should make this technology more affordable with time.

10.3. Dealing with Resistance to Change

Resistance to change is a common issue when integrating any new technology into existing business models. Workers familiar with existing systems may resist adopting VR, as it requires them learning new skills and adapting to different ways of working.

To tackle this resistance, businesses must illustrate the benefits of VR clearly. Highlighting how VR can make employees' tasks easier or how it can streamline processes can help to mitigate resistance. Management should also involve employees in the implementation process, seek their input, and address their concerns to foster a positive environment for change.

10.4. Device Durability and Dependability

The durability and dependability of VR devices are also critical considerations. Devices need to be robust, especially for applications in challenging environments like warehouses or outdoor logistical operations. Also, they should be consistent in their performance.

VR device manufacturers are continually improving the durability of their products. There is a growing trend of rugged VR equipment designed specifically for industrial use. Investing in these robust solutions and regular maintenance can ensure the dependability of the devices.

10.5. VR and Cyber Security

Cybersecurity threats pose a significant barrier to the adoption of VR technology. With the integration of VR, supply chain systems become more connected, increasing their vulnerability to cyber-attacks.

Firms need to augment their cybersecurity strategies when integrating VR. This may involve incorporating VR-specific security measures, regular system audits, and raising awareness about cyber threats among the employees. Collaboration with tech firms specializing in cybersecurity can yield significant advantages in this respect.

10.6. Establishing Standards and Regulations

Inconsistent standards and regulations for VR technology can also pose adoption difficulties. Lack of uniform guidelines for the safe and ethical use of VR, or how to effectively integrate it within existing processes, can slow its adoption.

For this, industry influencers and VR providers should work in tandem to establish standards and regulations for VR use within the logistics sector. Existing technological and safety standards may be based upon until these standards evolve.

The road to VR adoption in logistics and supply chain management is fraught with challenges. Yet, with a strategic approach to overcoming these barriers - including the ones highlighted in this discussion - it's entirely feasible and, indeed, desirable. The potential benefits to process optimization, efficiency improvement, and overall logistical performance make pushing past these barriers a worthy endeavour. Like most paradigm shifts, it requires commitment, strategic foresight, and an appetite for meaningful innovation.

Chapter 11. Virtual Reality: Future Trends and Possibilities

From its roots as a gaming gimmick, Virtual Reality (VR) has developed into a revolutionary tool with immense potentialities in various sectors, including Logistics and Supply Chain Management. By offering the advantages of increased efficiency, precision, and the opportunity for enhanced productivity, VR has firmly situated itself as an unignorable influencer in the logistics sector. Let's explore the future trends and possibilities of VR in the industry.

11.1. The Advancement of Virtual Prototyping

Virtual prototyping is heralding a new age in supply chain and logistics management. This technology allows companies to design, test, and perfect all aspects of their operations before turning them into reality. With the capability to minimize errors and unnecessary costs, virtual prototyping will become an industry standard for companies aiming to optimize their logistics workflow.

Previously, logistics planners used 2D models and statistical data to plan warehouses, dockyards, and shipping lanes; a process that could lead to oversights as it lacked actual spatiotemporal experience. However, VR is allowing these professionals to experience these scenarios in life-like three dimensions, making the planning and prototyping process more efficient, accurate, and meaningful.

11.2. Enhanced Training and Skill Development

With the advent of VR, there has been a noticeable shift in how companies train their workforce. VR provides immersive, repeatable, and safe scenarios for workers to hone their skills, from operating heavy machinery to executing delicate procedures.

In essence, VR can simulate any environment, either recreating real-world conditions or creating settings that are too risky or expensive to replicate, such as emergency scenarios. This aspect renders VR technology invaluable for safety and emergency training, as well as technical skill development, in the logistics sector.

11.3. Strengthened Warehouse Management

Warehouse management stands to gain significantly from VR technology. VR can provide an overview of the complete warehouse, allowing managers to observe real-time progress, regulate material flows, and identify potential problems from the convenience of their office.

In addition, VR visuals can be used for inventory management. Personnel can "see" inventory in real-time, allowing for swift and accurate updating. With VR technology, warehouse management can achieve unprecedented levels of coordination and efficiency.

11.4. Improved Maintenance and Repair

The maintenance and repair of machinery and equipment form a significant part of logistics companies' expenses. VR technology is set to change this drastically. Through Augmented Reality (AR), a subset of VR, companies can now have 'X-ray vision' - this allows technicians to 'see' inside machinery without dismantling it, saving time and cost on routine maintenance and troubleshooting procedures.

11.5. The Rise of Remote Collaboration

With the capacity to create immersive, collaborative environments, VR makes it possible for employees located in disparate geographical locations to work together, virtually, in real-time. This advancement could mean substantial savings in travel costs, quicker decision-making processes, and a more aligned, collaborative workforce, no matter where they are based physically.

Each of these advancements is a testament to the substantial potential VR holds for the logistics and supply chain industry. However, technology, like everything else, comes with its own set of challenges and limitations.

11.6. Challenges and Limitations of VR Tech

Despite its undeniable potential, VR technology is not without constraints. Some of the overarching challenges in the implementation of VR in logistics include high initial investment, user resistance due to unfamiliar technology, possible health issues like dizziness or disorientation caused by extended VR usage, and the need for robust, high-speed internet to deliver satisfactory VR experiences.

Organizations need to develop a clear understanding of these challenges while planning the integration of VR into their logistical processes. By anticipating these potential stumbling blocks, they can mitigate them and smooth the path for technological adoption.

11.7. Looking Ahead

As we stand on the brink of a new era in logistics and supply chain management, it is evident that VR technology holds profound potential to transform the way we think about and conduct logistical operations. The future trends and possibilities of VR in logistics span the spectrum from virtual prototyping, enhanced employee training, intensified warehouse management, to improved maintenance protocols and increased remote collaborations.

However, like any new technology, VR too comes with its share of challenges and limitations that organizations need to take into account. By approaching these challenges with strategic foresight and a well-thought-out approach, the future of VR in logistics and supply chain management looks bright, efficient, and most importantly, transformative. Investing in this technology today can set organizations up to traverse the logistics landscape of tomorrow with ease and ambition.